IMAGES
of America

PORTUGUESE
COMMUNITY
OF SAN DIEGO

D1604043

BELLE OF PORTUGAL CHRISTENING, 1937. This vintage photograph shows the elegance and beauty of a tuna boat christening celebration during the 1930s. The *Belle of Portugal* was built by Lawrence Oliver at Campbell's machine company and tragically sank in January 1967. It was customary for a family member to break a bottle on the bow before launching. Pictured from left to right are Doris Oliver, Mary Rosa, and Lucille Medina. (Courtesy of the Portuguese Historical Center.)

ON THE COVER: THE *SÃO JOÃO*, 1930s. She is an icon representing the powerful fishing industry the Portuguese, along with the Italian and Chinese communities, once captured and dominated. This vessel sponsored the 1938 festa with Mary F. Rebelo as queen. She proudly raised a flag in honor of her roots while the crew boldly faced adversity on the seas to bring home success in their new motherland. São João, on Pico Island in the Azores, holds a spectacular blessing of the fleet in mid-January. (Courtesy of the Portuguese Historical Center.)

IMAGES
of America

PORTUGUESE COMMUNITY OF SAN DIEGO

WITHDRAWN

The Portuguese Historical Center
with Donna Alves-Calhoun

ARCADIA
PUBLISHING

Published by Arcadia Publishing
Charleston SC, Chicago IL, Portsmouth NH, San Francisco CA

Printed in the United States of America

Library of Congress Control Number: 2009900017

For all general information contact Arcadia Publishing at:
Telephone 843-853-2070
Fax 843-853-0044
E-mail sales@arcadiapublishing.com
For customer service and orders:
Toll-Free 1-888-313-2665

Visit us on the Internet at www.arcadiapublishing.com

This book is dedicated to the spirited Portuguese men and women
who came before us and pioneered a more affluent life in San Diego.
Through these photographs the reader will travel their journey to a place
and time of strength, devotion, and persistence for a new homeland.

CONTENTS

ACKNOWLEDGMENTS

The Portuguese Historical Center (PHC) would like to thank first and foremost all benefactors past and present who have donated photographs and artifacts to the center so as to archive our history. We would also like to thank those that believed in our mission to preserve our heritage by supporting the center in all its endeavors. Thanks to all the contributors to this publication and their assistance, including, in no specific order: Tom Cesarini, St. Agnes Catholic Church, Fr. Mel Collier, Elsie Spondike, Helen Evans, Joe De Melo, John D. Brown, Aldina Brown Alves, Louann Sabatini, Lionel Vargas, Belmira Gonsalves, Matt and Kelly Madruga, Mary Pereira, Zita Lira, Gertrude Lauriano, Delores Madruga, Phyllis Rose, Joao's Tin Fish, Sal and Lucille Freitas, Deutilde Varley, Louise Virissimo, Delores Luz, Cathy Silva Dellenbach, Gayle Frank, Barbara Hosaka, Elsa Machado, Cecilia Santos, Mary and Leo Correia, and Carlos Silva. A special thanks goes to the all the directors of the Portuguese Historical Center for their help, support, dedication, and commitment to this project: Therese Garces, Rosemarie Silva, Diana Balelo, Daniel Silva, Virginia Corriea, Mary Giglitto, Aldina Alves, Shirley Virissimo, Andrea Da Luz, Barbara Moffat, Caprice Ribero-Virissimo, and Jordan Lubauch.

I would like to thank Debbie Seracini at Arcadia Publishing, who was very instrumental and patient in helping me write this book from the beginning to the end.

Heartfelt thanks and gratitude goes to PHC director Shirley Virissimo for her incredible dedication, guidance, and creativity in researching and designing this book with me. I would also like to thank my beautiful family for their support and patience during this venture. Without Craig, Louann, and Sydney it would have never been possible. I give my gratitude to attorney August Felando for his expertise and assistance regarding the YP and tuna industry. A big thank you goes to Jimmy Lira Jr., who provided valuable information and photographs for the tuna seiner history.

All proceeds of this book will go to support the Portuguese Historical Center in Point Loma; the center can be contacted at www.phcsandiego.org or 619-223-8895. Unless otherwise noted, all images appear courtesy of the Portuguese Historical Center.

INTRODUCTION

During the 14th century, Portuguese navigators dominated the world in sea exploration while charting courses and achieving unprecedented maritime discoveries. This became known as Portugal's Golden Age. European kings and queens commissioned many Portuguese explorers, such as Bartolomeus Dias, Vasco de Gama, and of course João Rodrigues Cabrilho, to declare territory in the New World for their kingdoms. In 1542, when Cabrilho landed at Ballast Point and discovered a picturesque bay surrounded by a grand peninsula, he had unknowingly uncovered a gold mine that would some day be renamed San Diego. It was commonly assumed that the Portuguese immigrated to the United States only to become prosperous before retreating back to their nation. That reflection promptly changed as they experienced a taste of great independence along with an improved quality of life. From that point on, the Portuguese resolved that America would become their new motherland.

Those who were fishing on the East Coast merged with those coming from the Azorean and Madeira Islands to continue their trade on the West Coast. Early fishing was courageously done by a simple hook and a line with live bait for chum. In 1910, a group of 15 families, along with a man named Frank Silva, a native of Cabo Verde, assembled at a home in La Playa to give thanks and praise to the Holy Spirit and celebrate Pentecost Sunday as they had done in their homeland. It is a tradition that allegedly traces back to the 1500s during the reign of Queen Isabel, married to King Dinis of Portugal, who was known for her humanity and immense faith in the Holy Spirit. It is here where San Diego's "Feast of the Divine Holy Spirit" began; an Old World tradition was re-created, and Rose Silva became their first queen. In 1910, the first Festa Do Divinio Espirito Santo was commemorated in San Diego. Because the Holy Spirit was the center of this blessed ceremony, the families felt it would be fitting to purchase the first sterling silver crown, which came with a scepter and adorned a dove symbolizing the Holy Spirit. The crown has a double importance; it first gives absolute dominion and reverence to the Holy Spirit and also gives honor to the royalty of Queen Isabel of Portugal, who decreed that Pentecost Sunday should be observed in honor of the Holy Spirit and should be associated with helping the poor. This celebration of Pentecost Sunday continued until 1915, when the community grew too large to house all who wanted to participate.

A desire to maintain this newly improvised folklore caused these families to acquire a piece of land on Addison Street, which would become a permanent residence for future festas and has survived to the present. In 1922, a man named M. O. Medina became president of the festa, and with immense humanity, kindness, and strength, a community came together and built a chapel, or *capela*, to house the newly purchased crown, or *coroa*, where it could be displayed and offerings could be made during prayer. Under the direction of three Portuguese men—John Lucas, a mason; Frank Brown, a painter; and Joseph Athaide, a carpenter—along with a fisherman from each Portuguese vessel, they assembled other influential people and constructed the chapel, which still remains in existence today.

Soon after, it was apparent that a larger facility to house the community's growing population was inevitable, and M. O. Medina made it his quest to travel up the coast to rustic areas and unpaved roads where Portuguese immigrants resided in the hopes of donations for the Portuguese Hall. It was not long before several prominent citizens donated sizeable amounts, and thereafter the passion burned into the entire community. The local fishermen donated 50¢ per ton from their pay: half for the building of the hall and half for their new church, St. Agnes. San Diego became known as the tuna capital of the world from the early 1930s up until the late 1970s. Well over 40,000 inhabitants became personnel of the new tuna industry, and 80 percent of families in the United States were serving tuna. San Diego's tuna industry was ranked third in the city's economy.

The Portuguese community reached out into the city and grew graciously along with it. In 1935, the world's fair came to San Diego for a second time, and Balboa Park hosted the grand exposition. Many citizens came to participate in the fair and view the stunning building that housed Portugal's exhibit. The House of Pacific Relations was founded in 1935, and international cottages were formed to showcase different ethnic backgrounds and customs. Portugal became a charter member and occupied one of the original cottages for many years. Several dairy farms also developed in Mission Valley, and some Portuguese citizens joined in that venture as well.

In 1941, the community had grown considerably, as had the fishing fleet. Larger and more efficient vessels were being constructed, and greater demands on and separation of the families were expected. The weather could be very hazardous, putting great strains on the boats as well. San Diego tuna boats were taken shortly after Pearl Harbor in December of 1941. The government ordered the fleet to leave fishing grounds and head for port. Ten vessels entered the Panama Canal Zone, and the U.S. Navy acquired the use of these boats. In 1942, the U.S. Navy decided that the bigger tuna boats in the community would be very beneficial in their fight during World War II. The local fleet became the Yard Patrol, fondly called "YPs" or "Yippie Boats." Playing an important part in the war, YPs were responsible for transferring food, troops, and supplies in the South Pacific. In 1946, the surviving majority of the boats were transformed back to fishing boats and former owners were allowed to purchase them back. At this time, large corporations bought out the canneries and began to consolidate the industry and became partners with the fisherman and boat owners.

As the United States grew and the fleet aged, the demands increased on the tuna industry to provide more and compete with the foreign trade. It was time for a change, and purse seining quickly evolved. Changing to more powerful engines (that could cover 3,000 miles without refueling), hydraulic power blocks, and nylon nets a mile long brought the fleet into the 20th century. Capt. Harold Medina, along with the Portuguese tuna industry, developed the Medina Panel, which helped greatly to protect the dolphin. Much like their great navigators, the Portuguese people have always maintained a sense of fortitude and boldness for exploration, which in turn preserved their heritage for many decades. Though the tuna industry has long since disappeared in San Diego, the effects of the trade will always remain a significant piece of San Diego's history. Today second and third generations of families continue the tradition of tuna fishing. The foundation of the Portuguese community and its people will always be remembered and cherished by its once impressive fleet and their genuine devotion to the Holy Spirit.

One

DISCOVERING A

NEW BEGINNING

EXPLORER JOÃO RODRIGUES CABRILHO.
Commemorated for his exploration
and discovery of California, in 1993
the U.S. Postal Service honored
Cabrilho with a 29¢ stamp. One of
his many landings included Ballast
Point in 1542, claiming new territories
for Spain. He unknowingly started
the arrival of Portuguese immigrants
with the hopes of a new life in a land
of great opportunity decades later.

Explorer of
California
1542

29
USA

Juan Rodríguez
CABRILLO

EARLY IN THE 20TH CENTURY. A great blend of Portuguese immigrants emigrated from the mainland of Portugal, as well as the Azorean and Madeira Islands, and started a move toward the United States. Arriving in several areas of the East Coast, they produced a new and diverse mix of traditions, folklore, and faith. Entering through Bar Harbor and Ellis Island, many remained on the East Coast until they had the means to venture west. Shortly thereafter, a new wave of movement began toward an area in California known as San Diego, and the foundation of the Portuguese community there was quickly set in motion.

Lages Whaling Station. The Portuguese tradition of fishing began with whalers that hunted the large mammal for oil for many generations. It is a custom that followed the Portuguese to the East and West Coasts of America. Two men are stopping to take a photograph with a whale, or *balea*, that was caught off the local waters of Pico, Azores, in the town of Lages. Whaling was an essential way of life, but it also a dangerous occupation, and many were injured during the hunts. (Courtesy Joe De Melo.)

The Frank-Machado Marriage, 1920s. Emigrating from the island of Madeira, Portugal, this couple eventually settled in San Diego's Portuguese community to join the tuna industry. (Courtesy of Gayle Frank.)

THE UNITED STATES OF AMERICA

CERTIFICATE OF NATURALIZATION

No. C-5450559

Application No 108-12

Personal description of holder as of date of issuance of this certificate Age 58 *years; sex* Female
complexion dark *color of eyes* brown *; color of hair* blk.-gray *height* 5 *feet* 2 *inches;*
weight 140 *pounds; visible distinctive marks* none
Marital status married *former nationality* Portugal

Anna Fernandes Francisco
(Complete and true signature of holder)

Be it known that ANNA FERNANDES FRANCISCO
residing at 1179 Willow St., San Diego, California
having applied to the Commissioner of Immigration and Naturalization for a Certificate of Naturalization and having proved to the satisfaction of the Commissioner that (s)he was naturalized by the Superior Court of California, in and for the County of San Diego, at San Diego, California, on May 29, 1942.

Seal

Now Therefore, in pursuance of the authority contained in Section 3431 of the Immigration and Nationality Act, this Certificate of Naturalization is issued this 14th *day of* January *in the year of our Lord nineteen hundred and* fifty-eight *and of our Independence the one hundred and* eighty-second *and the seal of the Department of Justice affixed pursuant to statute.*

IT IS A VIOLATION OF THE U. S. CODE (AND PUNISHABLE AS SUCH) TO COPY, PRINT, PHOTOGRAPH, OR OTHERWISE ILLEGALLY USE THIS CERTIFICATE.

212626

COMMISSIONER OF IMMIGRATION AND NATURALIZATION

DEPARTMENT OF JUSTICE

FORM N-570 (REV 5-1-57)

NATURALIZATION. The naturalization process was tedious and long. Sometimes it could take up to 10 years to receive citizenship, and documentation was very important to acquire jobs and status as an American. Shown here are the naturalization papers of Anna Fernandes Francisco. (Courtesy of Delores Luz.)

THE DA SILVA FAMILY. Originating in Pico, Azores, the Da Silva family had four daughters that all immigrated to the United States and established their lives in San Diego. Often siblings were left behind with the parents until one could send for them at a later date. All four Da Silva sisters are pictured at left when they reunited in Pico, Azores, to visit with their parents for the summer festas. From left to right are (first row) João Da Silva and Isabel Da Silva; (second row) Isabel Bettencourt, Maria Emilia Brown, Inez Rosa, and Isauda Da Silva. (Courtesy of Maria Melo.)

MARIA EMILIA DA SILVA.
Immigrating to the United States
in 1920 at the age of 17, Maria
Emilia sailed on the SS *Roma*
from Pico Island in the Azores.
These were her immigration
papers at the point of entry
through Ellis Island. Her parents
arranged for a Portuguese
family with a boardinghouse
in Gloucester, Massachusetts,
to become her sponsors, while
she took employment in the
Universal Coat Factory and
later worked at the Gorton's
Fisheries. (Author's collection.)

THE SS ROMA. This steamship was built for the Fabre Line in 1902 and ran a Mediterranean–New
York service. Weighing 5,291 gross tons with a steam triple expansion engine, twin screws, and a
double mast and funnels, she proudly housed 54 first-class and 1,400 third-class passengers. Many
Portuguese immigrants embarked on this vessel in route to America. (Author's collection.)

THE MANUEL MADRUGA FAMILY, 1885. Immigrating to United States in 1885 from the Azorean Islands, Manuel Madruga, his wife, and their children became the first documented Portuguese family to settle in San Diego. After arriving, Manuel pursued a life on the sea as a fisherman. Their first house was located on the peninsula area that eventually became known as La Playa of San Diego.

FRY (FERRIERA) FAMILY, 1900S. Many families immigrated to Northern California before heading to San Diego for the tuna fishing industry. They settled in rural areas like Visalia, Tulare, and Hanford. The Fry family is seen here on their farm in Visalia leaning against their antique automobile prior to relocating to San Diego. From left to right are Mary, Barbara, Lucy, Amelia, Delores, and Benjamin. (Courtesy of Helen Evans.)

THE BALELO-FRANCISCO WEDDING, 1925.
Adam Balelo and Mary Francisco were
married in Lowell, Massachusetts. After
several years on the East Coast, they
immigrated to San Diego to take a turn
at the fishing industry. Adam became
the owner of the bait boat *Ocean Pearl*,
and Mary worked in the High Seas Tuna
cannery. Emigrants from the Madeira
Islands found the mild climate in San
Diego very similar to their homeland.
(Courtesy of Delores Madruga.)

THE MEDINA WEDDING. Mary and
Machado Medina were married in
San Diego in 1922. Machado was
the brother of M. O., Joe, Frank,
Joaquin, and Fernando. All the
brothers became very successful boat
owners and helped pioneer the tuna
industry. Mary became the choir
director and piano accompanist
at St. Agnes for many years and
contributed beautiful music to the
mass with her voice and piano playing.
Mary was a piano accompanist
at Saint Agnes and the S.P.R.S.I.
lodge for many years. (Courtesy
of Marge Medina Amptman.)

POINT LOMA'S FIRST SCHOOL. Roseville Grammar School was constructed in the early 1900s and established in 1906 in La Playa on Byron Street in Point Loma. This school gave the Portuguese children living in the area a chance for an education. The class below is in session in 1906, and this is the first class picture taken at the new school. (Both courtesy of St. Agnes Catholic Church.)

CABRILLO ELEMENTARY SCHOOL, 1922. The first kindergarten class poses with its teacher on the new Cabrillo site on Talbot Street, and the children's classroom was now attached to the school. This school remains open today and celebrated its 100th birthday in 2006. (Courtesy of Gertrude Lauriano.)

MARY, 1900s. Depicting a simple earlier time in San Diego history, this poignant photograph shows a woman documented only as Mary, who appears to be looking out to sea. (Courtesy of St. Agnes Catholic Church.)

A View of La Playa, 1906. This aerial view was taken looking south from the top of Fort Rosecrans during the early 20th century. Notice the dirt road that is now Rosecrans Street. The bay is quiet with little activity, Shelter Island does not exist at this time, and a horse and buggy was the mode of transportation.

Two

BUILDING THE
FISHERMAN'S FAITH
ST. AGNES CATHOLIC CHURCH

THE FIRST ST. AGNES CATHOLIC CHURCH. St. Agnes was blessed on March 14, 1908, and dedicated by Bishop Thomas James Conaty in 1911. This was the first church in the La Playa area that allowed the Portuguese community a place to worship. (Courtesy of St. Agnes Catholic Church.)

POINT LOMA'S MISSION CHURCH. St. Agnes (left) was considered a mission church along with Mary Star of the Sea and Sacred Heart in Ocean Beach. It was Father Masny who built this church in 1908, and it became the fifth Catholic Church in San Diego. The interior of the church (below) was constructed of wood and built by the men of the parish. Its altar displayed the statue of St. Agnes, and two side altars featured the statues of Our Lady of Good Voyage, the patroness of the fishing fleet, and the Sacred Heart. The altar in this picture was decorated for the 1920 festa. (Both courtesy of St. Agnes Catholic Church.)

FATHER MASNY. Father Masny (above) arrived in 1906 in the La Playa area to replace Father Ubach, who was believed to be last of the mission padres. The Old Adobe Chapel in Old Town, St. Joseph's Church in downtown, and our Lady of the Angels in uptown were already established in San Diego. Traveling by horse and buggy, he covered several church communities as a minister. Working for 31 years with the Catholic community, Father Masny (below) became very close to its parishioners and founded mission churches as well as parishes throughout San Diego. (Both courtesy of St. Agnes Catholic Church.)

THE FIRST ST. AGNES CHOIR, 1911. Music played a significant role during mass. The majority of the congregation was of Portuguese descent, which kept them in tune with their homeland. Mass was sung in Latin. (Courtesy of St. Agnes Catholic Church.)

THE LADIES OF ROSEVILLE. Pictured is the La Playa peninsula in the background shortly after the beginning of the 20th century. Looking north, the church is on the left and the Roseville School is on the right. A group of parishioners pose for a picture after Sunday mass. (Courtesy of St. Agnes Catholic Church.)

THE NEW ST. AGNES, 1933. As the Portuguese community grew, so did the need for a larger structure, and 15 boats saved money to build a new one. The fisherman pledged 25¢ per ton of fish and many donated their labor to build a new St. Agnes. Individuals also made *promessa*, or promises, to help fund the new church with fund-raisers. Pictured here is a festa procession parading in front of the new St. Agnes Church on Evergreen Street. (Courtesy of St. Agnes Catholic Church.)

INSIDE ST. AGNES. A 16th-century Mediterranean-style church was designed, and the bell tower embraces a statue of Our Lady of Good Voyage, crowned with an illuminated cross that could be seen by the men out at sea. The new altar became a stunning backdrop for wedding photographs. St. Agnes was finally dedicated on May 4, 1934, by Bishop John Joseph Cantwell. (Courtesy of Virginia Correia.)

FR. MANUEL ROSE. Father Rose arrived at St. Agnes in 1933 at the request of M. O. Medina and became the first priest to preach the mass in Portuguese. According to parish records, he was a very social man in the community and made visits to the sick in their homes. Father Rose was given a small sailboat for enjoyment and often was seen sailing out to the lighthouse. (Courtesy of St. Agnes Catholic Church.)

FIRST CROWNING, 1934. Queen Lucy Rogers Marciel Bowker became the first Festa Queen crowned in the new St. Agnes Church by Father Rose. Captured here on the steps of the new church is the daughter of Mr. and Mrs. Joe S. Rodgers. Sponsored by Consuelha and Manuel H. Freitas and the boat MV *Navigator*, the festa lasted two days, and four-year-old Louise Freitas carried the crown from the navigator's chapel up to the church. (Courtesy of Kelly and Mathew Madruga.)

FIRST WEDDING. Belmira Falante (above) became the first bride married in St. Agnes Parish by Father Rose when she wed Manuel Pançinha Gonsalves on June 1, 1933. Their reception was held at Veronica Falante's (the bride's mother) house on Canon Street in Point Loma. All guests attending the wedding received this souvenir photograph. The wedding party, seen below from left to right, includes (first row) Eleanor Drumond, Manuel Gonsalves, Avelino Gonsalves, Belmira and Manuel Pançinha Gonsalves, Mary Falante, Marie Santos, and Ollie Virissimo; (second row) Edith and Mary Coelho, Mary Rebelo, and unidentified; (third row) Joaquim Medina, Manuel Fernandes, Agusto Rebelo Silva, and unidentified. (Both courtesy of St. Agnes Catholic Church.)

VARLEY WEDDING, 1937. Deutilde Medina Varley is pictured here with her husband, Eddie Varley Sr., on their wedding day. A beautiful courtship started when Deutilde was living in Santa Clara on her parents' dairy farm and Eddie came up from San Diego to vacation with family. After many trips between cities, Deutlide relocated to Point Loma, where they were married in the new St. Agnes Church on July 7. Shortly after, Eddie started tuna fishing and served on YP 292 in World War II. The Varleys hosted the 1955 festa. (Courtesy of Deutilde Varley.)

MONISE NUPTIALS, 1920s. Mary and Matthew Monise Sr. shared vows in St. Agnes Catholic Church and started a very successful life together in Point Loma. Owning several tuna boats and local properties, Matthew also was one of the original directors of the new Portuguese Hall. Mary was involved in the community while serving during festas and decorating the chapel religiously with love. (Courtesy of Phyllis Monise Rose.)

FIRST HOLY COMMUNION. Customary to the Catholic tradition, the sacrament of Holy Communion is a religious passage that is held in very high regard. Many Portuguese children in the San Diego area were sent to Catholic schools because of the academic and religious emphasis. Pictured is a communion group at St. Agnes Catholic Church with girls wearing the traditional white dresses with veils and boys in suits with white bows on their arms. Holy Family Sisters (below) are a religious society of nuns formed to assist churches and schools during the 1930s, and they are still active in other areas today. (Above, courtesy of Sal and Lucille Freitas; below, St. Agnes Catholic Church.)

JOHN DOMINGOS (DE BRUM) BROWN JR., 1938. "Brownie," as he was nicknamed, a first-generation native of Point Loma of Azorean descent, receives his First Holy Communion. Growing up on Addison Street across from St. Agnes Church, the Brown home was always open to family and friends and hosted new immigrant families. Addison Street was later renamed Avenida de Portugal in tribute to the festa procession. (Courtesy of John D. Brown.)

LIONEL JOSEPH VARGAS, 1938. Nicknamed "Pineapple," Lionel was a frequent visitor to the Brown home and loved how the "doors were never locked." A first-generation San Diegan of Azorean descent, he became a tuna boat captain and eventually retired from the industry. This picture was taken in front of Clarence "Bulldog" Silva's home on the corner of Carleton and Locust Streets on his communion day. (Courtesy of John D. Brown.)

THE SACRAMENT OF CONFIRMATION, 1939. Delores Francisco Madruga is portrayed to the right on her confirmation day in front of her house on Fenelon Street in Point Loma. In this childhood home she grew up and raised her family; she still lives there today. Below, on the steps of St. Agnes, Monsignor Lawrence Forristal (left) and Bishop Charles Buddy (center) captured the moment with the class of 1939. Confirmation day was a time of celebration with family, friends, and godparents. These religious ceremonies bonded the community and its youth with dedication and faith. (At right, courtesy of Delores Madruga; below, St. Agnes Church.)

PORTUGUESE BOYS BAND, 1935–1936. The image above depicts a culture rich in music, which was an integral part of the community. Here young boys pose for a picture as the first Portuguese Boys Band in front of St. Agnes. In a very formal setting (below), Bishop Charles Buddy takes a dramatic picture during a festa celebration. Palm fronds were draped over the entrance to the church and a white satin runner was laid down in his honor. (Both courtesy of St. Agnes Catholic Church.)

THE LEGION OF MARY. This was an all-women's religious society that originated in Ireland. Its members pray daily to the Blessed Mother and are world-renowned. The St. Agnes chapter was started by Monsignor Forristal in 1933, and the club continues to this day. Pictured from left to right are (sitting) Mary Nunes and Belmira Gonsalves; (standing) Lorreta Costa, Raul Fernandes, Sybyl Hughs, Dottie Dring, Mary Isadoro, Mary Freitas, Juliet Silveira, Marie Pitta, Mario Mends, Mimi Falante, and Rev. Mel Collier. (Courtesy of St. Agnes Catholic Church.)

STO NOME DE JESUS. This Portuguese women's organization translates in English as "in the name of Jesus." Participating in church and community events was the primary focus, including marching in festas and helping in religious events. (Courtesy of St. Agnes Catholic Church.)

SAINT AGNES CHOIR, 1964. Music has always been an inspiration and support during the liturgy, singing for all community events and many years, uniting families and friends. Isabel Soares Medina became choir director prior to 1936, followed by Carl Ackerman, Mary Oliver, and Mary Machado Medina. Director Catherine Keary (second row, far right) is seen with the choir, which consisted of men and women of the parish. (Courtesy of St. Agnes Catholic Church.)

THE PORTUGUESE CHOIR. Pictured here is the choir that has been directed by Bina Camacho for many years, giving St. Agnes a cultural diversion of music during the Portuguese mass. (Courtesy of St. Agnes Catholic Church.)

ST. AGNES SCHOOL. St. Agnes became an official school in 1946 and primarily served the Catholic communities of La Playa, Roseville, Point Loma, and Ocean Beach. In 1948, the students playing on the school grounds, pictured above, decided to strike a pose. Built by the M. H. Golden Construction Company, St. Agnes opened its doors in 1946 and was dedicated by Bishop Charles Buddy. Led by Principal Sister Bonaventure, the Sisters of St. Joseph's of Orange taught at the school. Below, the 1962 class poses in front of St. Agnes before graduation. The school finally closed its doors in 1970. (Both courtesy of St. Agnes Catholic Church.)

THEN AND NOW. Pictured above is the 1933 St. Agnes Church with the old church attached facing Canon Street and used at that time as a rectory. The circular stained-glass window above the doors housed a beautiful crown. Below, St. Agnes is pictured in 2009 with the new rectory and expansion on the corner of Evergreen Street and Avenida de Portugal. Beautiful imported Irish stained-glass windows were installed. Notice how the steps have been altered to create two separate entrances. The priest of St. Agnes, Rev. Joseph Mel Collier, has served the Portuguese community for many years. Father Collier delivers mass in Portuguese and supports the community in all religious and social activities. (Both courtesy of St. Agnes Catholic Church.)

Three

THE FESTAS OF QUEEN ST. ISABEL

A QUEEN HONORED, C. 1920. Queen St. Isabel has been a form of strength and a religious foundation for the Portuguese people since her reign during the 14th century. Born on July 4, 1271, she represents a holy devotion and compassion through every Espirito de Santo Festa (Holy Spirit Feast), which has become San Diego's oldest religious ethnic celebration and has been held for over 700 years. Queen St. Isabel, against the king's approval, delivered bread to the poor during times of great famine. Her husband, King Dinis, demanded she reveal what she was carrying. Roses miraculously fell to the ground. On Pentecost Sunday, her statue is carried with pride through the parade procession and is always adorned with fresh roses to symbolize "the miracle of the roses." (Courtesy of St. Agnes Catholic Church.)

AN OLD TRADITION, C. 1900. These images depict a young Roseville and the determination to continue traditions despite unforeseen obstacles and sometimes harsh conditions. Men proudly carried the flags of their old and new countries, and the community dressed in their Sunday best to watch the crowning of the queen. A procession to the church was the excitement of this festa, and everybody looked forward to the feast held on Penecost Sunday, the seventh Sunday after Easter. A coroa, or crown, was not used in the celebration until 1910, when it was purchased by Frank Silva and other community citizens. (Both courtesy of St. Agnes Catholic Church.)

QUEEN MARY AND PARADE, 1914.
Mary Miller Oliver was crowned Festa
Queen in the old St. Agnes Church at
the age of 15, and Joe Lawrence was
the *mordome*, or chairman, of the feast.
The crown placed upon Mary Oliver's
head, at right, was handcrafted of
elaborate sterling silver and symbolizes
the reign of Queen St. Isabel. Her
dress is a simplistic, form-fitting,
double-layered skirt. In the photograph
below, her procession parades north
on unpaved roads on Carleton and
Canon Streets. In the background,
a horse and buggy are pictured.

THE CABRILLO PAVILION, 1914. The first community hall in Point Loma was used to accommodate more people for the local festivities. It was located on Locust Street in Roseville and constructed by Mr. Brown (Brum). The hall was first used for seven years before a new and exclusive Portuguese Hall was erected due to the growing population.

MARY MONTEIRO RICKENBERG, 1918. Rickenberg, posing here, became Festa Queen in 1918 and remains one of the oldest figureheads symbolizing the true meaning of festa. Pictured at the top of the page is her procession on Pentecost Sunday. The crown is carried as she leads the parade up to St. Agnes Church with a grand Portuguese flag leading the way.

A TOAST TO THE KITCHEN STAFF, C. 1920. A festa wouldn't be complete without the hard work and dedication of the kitchen staff. These men and women are essential to the events that comprise the festa and work countless hours preparing and serving food. In the vintage image above, the kitchen staff takes a break to toast their efforts. From left to right are (first row) three unidentified; (second row, sitting) John Monise, Joaquin Xavier, Anthony Monise, John Lucas, Joe Monise, and Frank Silva; (third row) Mary Xavier, Mrs. Rita Monise, two unidentified, Frank Brown, and (sitting) Manuel Silva; (fourth row) three unidentified. Below, John Coelho (second from left) proudly poses with the cooking crew on a festa day in the 1930s. (Below, courtesy of Helen Evans.)

THE NEW UNITED PORTUGUESE SOCIEDADE DO ESPIRITO SANTO (U.P.S.E.S.) HALL, 1922. The new U.P.S.E.S. hall, seen above, was built in 1922 to replace the old Cabrillo Pavilion festa setting. Money was lent to the organization by Joe Rodgers and Manuel Corriea to purchase the property. The boats pledged the labor of one fisherman per boat to construct the chapel and hall. The capela was a miniature house built in the Emperio style that housed an altar to hold the crown. In the formal portrait at left are John Lucas, his wife Mary, and daughter Adelaide. John was a mason and one of the three men who constructed the chapel in 1922; he was also the caretaker of the hall. (At left, courtesy of Phyllis Rose.)

M. O. MEDINA, C. 1920. M. O. Medina and committee built the first U.P.S.E.S. Hall and Chapel, and he was elected as the first president. Collecting funds and working with other families in the Point Loma area, he helped raise money for the new hall. Medina remained president for over 40 years and became one of the respected leaders in the new community.

FESTA CHAIRMEN

M. O. Medina 1922-1929	M. M. Medina 1923	Frank P. Silva 1924-1936	M. S. Monise 1925	Joe S. Rogers 1926
Joe F. Sousa 1927	Manuel Medina 1928-1941	M. S. Soares 1930	Manuel F. Silva 1931	Mathew Monise 1932-1948
Joe Medina 1933-1940	M. H. Freitas 1934	M. G. Rosa 1935-1942	M. F. Correia 1937-1943	A. Francisco 1938
J. O. Medina 1939-1945	A. G. Rosa 1944	Augusto Silva 1946	Frank Medina 1947	

FESTA SPONSORS. Pictured here are the festa sponsors, or chairmen, from 1922, when M. O. Medina became the first hall president. This listing represents many prominent families and tuna boat owners who worked together to continue the tradition of festa for many years.

QUEEN OF THE NEW U.P.S.E.S. HALL, 1922. Hazel Ahaide Monise is with her sweet flower girls Gertrude Brown Lauriano (left) and Tillie Athaide DeGraca (right) on the steps of the new capela. The queen's hair is done with long ringlets and her cape is trimmed. It was common for royalty to carry flower petals in a lace pouch during this time. The women in the chapel doorway are very proud of their queen.

MARY LUCAS MONISE, C. 1920. Festa Queen Mary Monise is shown with her royal court. The Portuguese Society of Queen St. Isabel (S.P.R.S.I.) members who marched in the festas would wear their velvet-fringed *regalias*, or vests, displaying their lodge name. This royal court is shown standing in front of the hall. (Courtesy of Phyllis Rose.)

WOMEN IN THE FESTA, C. 1930. By the 1930s, the festas had grown and become an official parade. Sto Nome de Jesus is proudly walking as a religious society and holding the banners commonly used during this time period. Seen in front from left to right are Rosalina Fernandes, Mrs. Virissimo, Esther Coito (slightly behind), and Belmira Gonsalves; the angels are unidentified. These women became affluent citizens of the community and worked diligently in many areas. (Courtesy of St. Agnes Catholic Church.)

DRILL TEAM, 1929. In 1921, a drill team was organized by the Portuguese Protective Union of the State of California (U.P.P.E.C.) and joined the festa procession. In this vintage photograph, the 1929 drill team is posing in front of the capela on festa day. Notice that the area around the chapel is open for parking. Today it is only accessible from the front. (Courtesy of Virginia Correia.)

RIDING IN STYLE TO THE FESTA, c. 1920. Pictured from left to right, Johnny Athaide, Alice Silva, and James Brown are riding to the festa in this classic automobile and have stopped for a fun photograph on the corner of Canon and Rosecrans Streets. In the left background is George Leonard's grocery store, a favorite spot for provisions as well as Frizados Market on Carleton Street. (Courtesy Gertrude of Lauriano.)

H. G. KLAUCKE BLACKSMITH, c. 1920. During this festa procession, the queen is passing a local blacksmith shop in the neighborhood. Most Portuguese families at this time did not own automobiles, and some depended on this blacksmith for repair of their horse and buggies.

44

LITTLE FRIENDS, 1935. This charming little cortege is assembled on the steps of St. Agnes with the little queen. Pictured from left to right are (first row) Evelyn Medina and Lillian Gonsalves; (second row) Marge Medina, Loraine Monise (queen), and Genevieve Sebastian; (third row) Ms. Theodore, Laverne Monise, two unidentified, Virginia Xavier, and Lorraine Cardoso. Some of these little girls still remain friends today. (Courtesy of Marge Medina Amptman.)

LITTLE ANGELS, C. 1930. Angels have been a part of the festa since its inception, representing the religious aspect of the parade and reminding the people of their faith. Angel costumes were white and very simple, and they always escorted the queen. Delores Madruga (left) reminisced about when she and Mary Falante (right) took a rest on the steps of the Madruga home before the festa. (Courtesy of Delores Madruga.)

FESTA QUEEN ALICE SYLVIA MUCCI, 1932. Mathew C. and Mary Monise and the tuna vessel *Olympia* sponsored that year's festa, seen above. Those identified in the image are flower girl Phyllis Monise Rose (first row, center), side maid Gertrude Brown Lauriano (second row, second from left), Queen Alice Sylvia Mucci (second row, center), and side maid Adeline Silva Medina (second row, second from right). Below, a festa parade is leaving the Portuguese Hall and marching up to the church on Addison Street. A new, smaller hall was added to the existing hall (right) to accommodate the youth. Notice a tuna boat is in the distant bay, and the adjacent property across the street is vacant. (Below, courtesy Phyllis Rose and Gertrude Lauriano.)

THE LAST MARCH, 1932. Angels head up the above parade, and the queen follows after leaving the chapel at the corner of Scott and Addison Streets. Houses are more apparent, and cars line the streets having become more common. Note the addition of the band and its patriotic flag. The procession seen below marches north to the old St. Agnes Church seen in the distance. This would be the last march to the old church. An electric streetcar appears on Rosecrans Street (right), which was unpaved at the time. (Both courtesy of Phyllis Rose and Gertrude Lauriano.)

POSING FOR HISTORY, C. 1920. A piece of history is captured in this outstanding photograph depicting an entire group of proud Portuguese Americans in San Diego. The backdrop is the

A NEW ERA. This vintage image showcases a collection of automobiles lined up for a festa during

impressive capela and hall, which are decorated with palms customary of the Pentecost season for acting president Frank Silva's festa in 1924. (Courtesy U.P.S.E.S. Inc.)

the 1930s. (Courtesy of St. Agnes Catholic Church.)

A QUEEN'S COURT, C. 1930. A queen's court is comprised of maids to escort her, four *varas* (young girls) who carry poles to surround her, and flower girls who precede her. Note the different style of crowns the flower girls have adorned. On festa day, children were placed in front of the royalty in their white dresses.

INTRODUCTION OF THE LITTLE QUEEN, 1937. The little queen was introduced in the 1930s, and pictured here is Queen Ernestine Correia with her royalty on the steps of the capela. Posing from left to right are (first row) Alice, Gabriella Francisco, Queen Ernistine Correia, Lucy Francisco, and Aldina Brown; (second row) Lucille Cordozo; (third row) Lenora Texeira, George, and Jeannie. (Courtesy of Lucille Cordozo.)

QUEEN MARY CORREIA MARTIN, 1939. This beautiful royal court surrounds the queen (second row, center), and she is pictured with her side maids Rita Viera (left) and Helen Labruzzi (right) in front of the capela, which includes a king. The king was introduced in 1937, along with his sides, to the pageantry of the festa. It is said that vara poles (four poles tied together in a square) were used to keep the little king in line with the procession.

QUEEN MARGE MEDINA, 1941. Marge Medina Amptman became Festa Queen in 1941 and is posing here with friends and side maids Phyllis Monise Rose (left) and Genevieve Sebastian (right). Marge's father, Machado Medina, became an accomplished tuna fisherman and is pictured behind his daughter with the festa president's banner and a very proud smile. (Courtesy of Marge Medina Amptman.)

RITA MONISE, 1922. Rita Monise became the first head kitchen cook for the Portuguese Hall. She was a dedicated and committed individual, along with her coworkers, who took on the enormous task of preparing the festa meal. Many cooks followed Rita in this honored position: Florinda Neto, Maria Emilia Monise, Conceicao Athaide, Conceicao Virissimo, Rosella C. Monise, Elevina Neves, Mary Alice Oliver, Margaret Madruga, and Evelyn Silva Medina. (Courtesy of Phyllis Rose.)

A QUEEN'S BANQUET, C. 1940. The *sopas* meal for the 1940 festa was served in this facility of unknown origin. The queen is shown (center) seated amongst her guests instead of the traditional seating with a separate head table. Note the delicate beaded caps the side maids are wearing. (Courtesy of Delores Madruga.)

52

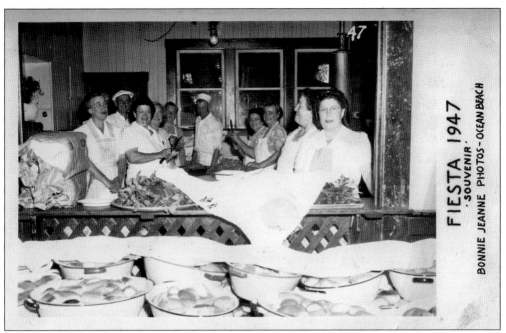

"Fiesta" Souvenirs, 1947. An Ocean Beach photographer named Bonnie Jeanne captured images and made souvenir postcards for the parade. Note the misspelling of "festa" as "fiesta," which was a common mistake. Sometimes roasting the meat was done at a local bakery because the hall did not have big enough ovens. It would take several days to prepare all the food necessary for the feast. (Courtesy of Virginia Correia.)

Blessing of the Workers. Fr. Nicholas Dempsey is blessing the workers and the festa meal as he holds the coroa over the pots of meat. This allows the workers to be blessed while everyone is attending high mass. It is customary for the queen to escort the father into the kitchen for this religious ceremony. "Father Nick" was loved by all in the community and socialized with the Portuguese peoples.

POSING WITH POTS, C. 1930. A group of women poses in the kitchen for a rare photograph smiling in their pretty aprons. During the process of the sopas meal, it could get very hot inside the kitchen and photographs were frowned upon. These women were the backbone behind the meal served in tradition of Queen St. Isabel and her dedication to the poor.

PORTUGUESE AMERICAN SOCIAL AND CIVIC CLUB, 1930s. Instituted in December 1940, this social club began meeting in 1941. Founders included Lawrence Oliver and Tony and Edna Madruga. The purpose of the club was to establish a social, civic, and cultural community for Portuguese Americans. Club members are seen here preparing sweet bread, which is a traditional bread of the Portuguese people.

FESTA SERVERS, C. 1930. Festa servers are lined up outside the preparation area of the kitchen with bowls ready to go out for the sopas meal. Meeting the demands of the parade crowd is a very challenging job. This image depicts generations of mothers, daughters, and granddaughters serving together. (Courtesy of Virginia Correia.)

CREATION OF THE CEILING CROWN, 1955. The addition of the crown to the hall was conceived by Edward and Deutilde Varley, and the crown was handmade by Eddie Varley Jr., Frank Medina Jr., and Andrew Silva. It was constructed of intricate glass pieces purchased by Deutilde and was hung from the ceiling. This festa was the first to return to the chapel for the rosaries.

MARY GIGLITTO, 1944. Mary is depicted as a Little Queen sitting for a portrait at the popular Vreeland studio. Growing up in Point Loma, she attended St. Agnes School and became a very accomplished member of the community. Mary was an elementary school teacher in the San Diego district and an emeritus president for the Cabrillo Festival who assists João Rodrigues Cabrillo on his many appearances. Currently she also serves as a director of the Portuguese Historical Center.

THE THREE SAINSTMEN, C. 1950. King Bobby Virissimo and sides Ollie Jr. (left) and Rick (right) Virissimo make a grand exit from church on festa day. Notice the crown, scepter, and plate made of flowers. These three boys attended Saint Augustine Catholic High School in San Diego.

56

THE YOUNGEST FESTA QUEEN, 1965. Cathy Silva Dellenbach (center), the daughter of Manuel A. Silva and Mary Silva, made festa history when she became the youngest queen at the age of 11. The Silva family is honored to have three generations of festa queens: Mary Ferreira Silva, Cathy Silva Dellenbach, and Lynnae Keltner. (Courtesy of Cathy Silva Dellenbach.)

THE PARASOL GROUP, 1940s. The Parasol Group has always brought a darling component to the parade. Little girls twirling their umbrellas are a delight for parents to watch and embrace. This is the age where children were introduced to their religious heritage and were encouraged to participate in the parade annually.

THE SIGN CARRIERS, 1969. The sign carriers are a crucial part of the parade, maintaining order and announcing the upcoming groups. The signs are more decadent as the royalty approaches and are handmade to color coordinate and compliment the groups. Edwin Alves and Steven Brown were chosen to carry the Infant of Prague sign for the 1969 festa. (Courtesy of Phyllis Rose.)

THE HOLY INFANT OF PRAGUE. Most of the time, an Infant of Prague is a young boy between the ages of two and four. The Infant carries a ball representing the world, and his two fingers are tied together for peace. Manny Lucas became the first Infant of Prague to be carried on a platform, which has now become tradition. The Shriners of the community are seen here carrying Pete Garces at the age of four. (Courtesy of Therese Garces.)

Santo Amaro. The Festa do Santo Amaro was founded in San Diego in 1939 by descendants of emigrants from Paul Do Mar on Madeira Island, Portugal. Santo Amaro's feast day is celebrated on January 15, and the descendants continue to honor their patron saint here in San Diego. Today the Festa do Santo Amaro is a nonprofit fraternal organization composed of persons of Portuguese descent and family members. Among its purposes is furthering the education and welfare of persons of Portuguese descent. Pictured here, Santa Amaro is being carried during festa in keeping with tradition.

Cabrillo Club. This club was organized for Californians of Portuguese descent, their spouses, and individuals interested in Portuguese culture. It was founded to honor the memory of João Rodrigues Cabrilho, promote Portuguese culture, improve the surrounding community through civic involvement, and provide financial assistance for Portuguese youth seeking a college education. The festa bazaars were started with the 1955 festa, and the first president was Matt Oliveira. Pictured is the booth that Cabrillo Club No. 16 hosts annually.

THE DOWNTOWN FESTAS. Do Festa do Espirito Santo was started in San Diego's downtown area by Lawrence and Mary Oliver. The parade was first held in 1921 and lasted until 1963. Our Lady of the Rosary Catholic Church on Columbia and Date Streets was used for the coronations. Portuguese citizens also contributed to the building of this church, and the altar was of an ornate old-world style. The spectacular gold crown, seen above, was donated to the University of San Deigo Immaculata and was placed in a chapel built by Lawrence Oliver, where it remains today. The queen below is leaving Our Lady of the Rosary Church with her court.

VISITING QUEENS. It was customary for the downtown festa to invite the Espirito Santo Queen from Point Loma to walk in their procession. One had to be asked, and it was an honor to represent the festival. Lillian Marie Brown (center) is attending the downtown parade and representing the 1954 Point Loma Festa. She is holding a bouquet of flowers instead of her crown and is not crowned in the high mass. (Courtesy of Shirley Virissimo.)

WHAT A PRETTY SIGHT. It is always delightful to see children participating in their heritage all dressed in white and with smiles on their faces. These darling little girls are carrying baskets as they march with their mothers following close behind. Parents are seen assisting their children as they guide them throughout the parade.

THE LONGEST PROCESSION, C. 1930. This striking image portrays the immensity of this charming group of little girls as it trails behind for what appears to be a mile. What a fabulous sight to behold as they stride toward the church.

LITTLE GIRLS. This captivating image conveys the funny and sometimes angry moments children have during a hot or long festa. In this classic photograph, one little girl is proudly posing while another is sneering. These are the times festa participants will remember best.

FESTA CELEBRATION, 1958. In the above festa, Little Queen Cynthia Alves (front row, fourth from the left) walks in procession, accompanied by her side maids and court. Shirley Ann Brown Virissimo (front row, third from the left) is a PHC director and wife of tuna captain Rick Virissimo. Below, Mary Oliver (standing, second from the left) serves the priest the sopas meal during the elaborate queen's luncheon held at the Balboa Park Club. Junior Queen Joanne Balelo is seen with her side maids, and Mrs. May Mitchell is serving her granddaughter and Little Queen Cynthia Alves. (Above, courtesy of Shirley Virissimo.)

A DEDICATED QUEEN, 1948. By 1947, the community had outgrown the old hall, and it was evident that new and more updated version needed to be constructed. After the hall's completion in 1948, a contest was held to find a queen for the dedication. Angie Viera is shown placed upon her throne as the queen of the new S.E.S. Hall. Her side maids are Hazel Gonsalves (right) and Lenora Texeira (left).

WEEKLY CORONATIONS, c. 1950. Starting seven weeks prior to Pentecost Sunday, six weekly queen coronations signify the seven gifts of the Holy Spirit. Each family receives the crown and hosts daily rosaries in their house until the subsequent Sunday, when a coronation is held to bless the weekly queen and the crown is passed to the next family. At the end of six weeks, the crown is returned to the president and publicly displayed for daily rosaries until Pentecost Sunday.

WEEKLY QUEENS, C. 1940. PHC director Aldina Alves (left image) poses for a portrait with her side maids, Eleanor Mitchell (left) and Eileen Vargas (right), for her weekly crowning. Aldina became Cabrillo Club No. 16's first financial secretary and currently serves on three boards, including the PHC. Today she remains very dedicated and active in the community. Virginia Correia (right image) was also crowned a weekly queen in St. Agnes Church and served as a U.P.S.E.S. and S.P.R.S.I. grand officer and PHC founder-director. Virginia also became a parliamentarian for many local clubs. (At left, courtesy of Aldina Alves; at right, Virginia Correia.)

BARBARA BALATORIE HOSAKA, 1959. Mr. and Mrs. Adrian Mauricio chose their niece Barbara to represent their crowning, and she is seen here with the festa crown. The daughter of Gilmore and Rita Balatorie, Barbara has been serving the community with dedication for many years. Being a U.P.S.E.S. president, director, and treasurer and Cabrillo Club No. 16 president keeps Barbara very active.

THE CORONATION, 1940. A festa queen's coronation is truly a sight to behold. Tradition and faith fill the air as she walks down the isle while the choir is singing the Portuguese "Alva Pomba" (Holy Ghost Hymn). She bows her head in grace as the priest crowns and blesses her by the Holy Spirit. It is a very proud and exceptional moment for any young queen. Queen Lucille Machado is wearing a traditional white dress and cape typical of this time period.

A BROCADE QUEEN, C. 1950. Brocade has always been considered a royal fabric. Intricately detailed patterns of gold and silver threads are woven throughout the material. This queen is carrying an unusually large but outstanding brocade cape in a stunning white-on-white pattern. The top of the cape, called a hood, usually stands up around the head. Note in this image that it is elegantly lying down.

A Miracle Queen, c. 1960. Cheryl Rose was truly a queen of faith who experienced the power of prayer first hand. Diagnosed at a young age with Hodgkin's disease, Cheryl had to undergo radiation treatments prior to her festa. The community prayed for her strength to complete the entire week of queen obligations. Their prayers were answered, and she miraculously walked the entire parade route without any assistance. The Knights of Columbus surround the queen with swords raised to afford her a grand entrance. (Courtesy of Phyllis Rose.)

The First Double Queens, 1994. Brenda and Jolene Jorge were the first to be crowned as double queens. It was said Jose Jorge could not choose upon which daughter to bestow the honor, and he was not in good health. The S.E.S. Hall granted his request to have the first double coronation. Their dresses were of museum quality and incredible elegance.

EIGHTY YEARS OF TRADITION. Festa presidents Matthew and Kelly Madruga made history when they sponsored the parade in 2006 in memory of Elsie Lira Cerny, seen above. Their daughters Loriana Marie (second row, far left) and Alyssa Ann (second row, far right) were crowned on the 80th anniversary of their great-grandfathers' festa in 1926. Joe S. Rogers is shown at left on his festa day with daughter Lucy Rogers (holding crown) and her court. Joe was responsible for loaning the money to the new U.P.S.E.S. board for the purchase of the hall property in 1921. (Both courtesy of Matthew and Kelly Madruga.)

EXCHANGING OF THE CROWNS, 1984. This ceremonial exchange from the outgoing queen to the new one has always been part of the festa tradition. It symbolizes the beginning of a new Pentecost year and queen. Evelyn Da Rosa Feliciano (left) is receiving the crown from Lisa Feliciano Pereira in front of the capela on a Saturday night. The queens will also exchange crowns in church.

THE FESTA PRESIDENT. Traditionally men exclusively wore the president's festa sash. In 2003, the honor of festa president was bestowed upon Gorete Correia. She made history and became the first woman in 93 years to host a festa, in memory of her late husband, Jose Carlos Correia. Pictured are Gorete (far left), displaying her sash with pride, and her double queens Chyrstal (first row, center) and Corinna (second row, center) as they pose with her court. Also pictured are (first row) side maids Jonique Joyner (left) and Alyssa Oliveira (right); (second row) side maids Nicole Avila (third from left) and Tayrn Joyner (second from right) and grand marshal Jose Guilherme Correia (far right).

PARADING PROUDLY. Frank Souza became the last boat owner to follow the festa tradition of anchoring in the bay on Shelter Island and illuminating his ship with lights. Boat captains and owners are seen here marching with pride during a parade procession. Each is wearing a sash stating their tuna vessel's name. These prominent men played a significant role in the Portuguese community and the tuna industry. From left to right are Joe Falante, Frank Correia, Ray Medeiros, unidentified, Chuck Gonsalves, A. Roland Virissimo, unidentified, Tony Rose, Al Ferreia, and John Silveira. Not shown are Manuel Grace and Frank Souza.

THE GRAND MARSHAL. The grand marshal is essential for the procession, as he keeps the order and pace of the parade. Usually a person of special importance is chosen for the honor bestowed by the festa president. The late John Lincoln Cerny is pictured here as the 2006 grand marshal. John served the tuna fleet as a captain and navigator. Later he went on to support the fleet with great pride as a marine supplier while managing San Diego Marine Hardware. (Courtesy of Cerny family.)

Four

EXTRAORDINARY
SEAMANSHIP OF THE
PORTUGUESE FLEET

MEN OF THE SEA, C. 1920.
Portuguese men have always
maintained exceptional navigation
and seamanship qualities that have
been handed down from father to
son for generations. These attributes
began with the great whaling days in
their homeland and were sustained
through the powerful purse seine
revolution that swept through the
tuna industry. The Portuguese fleet
developed cutting-edge techniques
and mastered the majestic sea.

PORTUGUESE DORY MEN, 1900S.
The Portuguese started out as whalers and manned tall ships before the tuna industry took off. Author Manuel Lester is pictured on the right. He sailed as a dory man on the Gloucester schooners in the late 1920s. Note the size of the main boom above their heads.

CHRISTENING OF THE SANTO AMARO, 1930. The decorative launchings of the old boats, with anchors and wreaths made of beautiful garlands, were a sight to behold. Patriotic flags lined the platform as Mary Freitas launched and christened the *Santo Amaro*. With a combination of 12 owners, this bait boat became one of the fleet's highliners.

SAN DIEGO MARINE CONSTRUCTION COMPANY. As one of the oldest marine construction companies in San Diego, it became a leading boat facility for boat owners in its day. Ranging from ferries and YP vessels to tuna seiners, it had a diverse range of services for boat owners' needs. Above, an all-wooden boat is being framed out. Below, the ferry *Virginia* and a double-masted schooner named *Ramona* are being worked on in dry dock.

SAN DIEGO PACKING COMPANY, 1914. Joseph Azevedo founded the San Diego Packing Company, seen above, located at the base of Dickens Street. He revolutionized the way tuna was processed, and his was the world's first facility to can tuna. Below, he is seen here third from the left at the packing facility. (Both courtesy of Phyllis Rose.)

THE SALTING HOUSES, C. 1900. These La Playa Bay salt-drying houses were used to dry out fish during the packing process. Rows of wood planks support the fish as they are laid out to dry. This method of preserving tuna was the only means of transporting fish to Portuguese communities in California. (Both courtesy of Phyllis Rose.)

THE DORY BOAT, 1900s. By the 1890s, the tuna industry was obsolete. The Portuguese fished short day trips on small dory boats due to the lack of refrigeration. Catching fish by hook and line was the traditional method. While fishing in small boats, they kept close to the peninsula. The *America* is pictured next to the rocky cliffs on a day trip.

THE BEVERLY, 1943. Built by Kettenburg Marine, the 38-foot jig and bait boat was designed to catch albacore tuna and swordfish and was purchased by Capt. João Beñto in 1945. He and son John Domingos Brown became the top commercial swordfishers for five consecutive years, catching 349 harpooned swordfish in one year. John later purchased two swordfish boats, *Bento* and *De Brum*. His son Steve Brown was taught the art of swordfishing and later became a captain. (Courtesy of Shirley Virissimo.)

WHAT A CATCH! This massive tuna was caught on the tuna boat *Elsinore* and proudly hoisted up for a once-in-a-lifetime photograph. The 100-pound tuna was a fisherman's dream, and Jose Jorge (left), Joe De Melo (center), and Manuel Camara pose with pride. These men were career fishermen and remained best friends during their prominent careers. (Courtesy of Joe De Melo.)

MV ATLANTIC, c. 1926. Built by Campbell Shipyard for owner M. O. Medina, this 112-foot bait boat was cutting-edge technology at the time. Refrigeration was installed in the holds so that the vessel could make long-range trips. Originally it was built as a flush-deck boat but was improved to a raised-deck vessel of 150 tons in 1930. The *Atlantic* had a 300-horsepower diesel engine.

The Crew that Built the Palomar, c. 1900. The incredible picture above, taken at San Diego Marine Construction, shows the manpower required to a build a clipper ship of this size. All the men gather for a photograph to show off their prize work. Below, the *Palomar* is up on the ways so the men can work underneath her. Note the old scaffolding and the dingy in the water.

CAMPBELL MACHINE COMPANY, 1920s, AND THE BELLE. The *Belle of Portugal* was built in 1937 by the Campbell Machine Company at the Campbell Shipyard (above), was 142 feet in length, and carried 350 tons. She was requisitioned and served in the U.S. Naval Reserve during World War II for three and a half years. The *Belle* (below) is seen on her trial-run voyage in San Diego Bay with family and friends. Tragically she caught fire and sank in January 1967, but the crew was spared.

THE ART OF POLE FISHING.
Catching tuna with bamboo rods and barless hooks was a job that required endurance, strength, and stamina. Sometimes it was a very long day, with backbreaking hours pulling in 30- to 70-pound tunas. The chummer was protected from soaring squid by a canopy built over the bait area. A pad socket was also developed for the bamboo pole to rest in and protect the fishermen from the violent force of the fish. In the 1950s, helmets were designed and used for protection. Sometimes weather was highly unpredictable and uncooperative, and men would be almost submerged under water. Both of these images clearly demonstrate the risk involved to yield a great catch.

FOUR-POLE TUNAS AND A POSE. Pole fishing was incredibly dangerous and called for an individual with strong resilience to maintain balance for hours in the racks. Each man was required to work close with other crew members. In some cases, a third or even a fourth pole was attached to help stabilize very large tunas. Distinctive fishing gear consisted of large rubber boots, a pad pocket for the pole, and a helmet. The image to the right is an example of the teamwork it takes to haul a large tuna up, over, and into the boat. Below, Jack Theodore is showing off a very large tuna with a glorious smile. (At right courtesy of João's Tin Fish.)

MV LUSITANIA, 1927. Built by Campbell Machine Company for owner and captain Manuel Rosa in 1927, the *Lusitania* was a larger tuna clipper with the capability to fish long-range in the Eastern Pacific Ocean. This started a wave of long-range boats. Above, Captain Rosa (top row, second from left) is seen with his crew. Below, the *Lusitania* is docked in the San Diego Bay before a trial run with family and friends.

THE *PARAMOUNT*, C. 1940. The Madruga brothers, Hank, John, Edward, and Joe, became expert seamen and knowledgeable in tuna boat management. Their accomplishments as a group and as individuals have been brilliant. Tuna boat owner Mr. Gonsalves (Gann) is attributed with giving Joe his first opportunity at running a vessel. In 1938, Joe became the youngest captain in the tuna fishing fleet at the age of 18, and he handled the responsibility with great skill. Joe privately owned numerous tuna boats during his career and provided opportunities to many other captains as well. Pictured above is the crew of the *Paramount*, and below Joe Madruga Sr. and son Joe take a moment for a photograph.

MARY E. PETRICH, C. 1940. This vessel was built by Mr. Petrich and captained by Jose Vierra Alves. In its day, the *Mary E. Petrich* (left) was the fastest boat in the fleet, and the Galapagos Islands off Ecuador was her favorite fishing spot. Captain Alves and the crew are credited with donating the first Galapagos turtles to the San Diego Zoo. The bronze statues of these enormous turtles can be seen today in the children's zoo. In addition, flamingos and exotic fish were also donated with the zoo's appreciation. Below, the crew is, from left to right, (first row) Johnny Sorsie and Eddie Alves; (second row) Gus Goularte, John Brown, Frankie Mitchell, Charlie Motta, Thomas Enos, and Johnny Gomes. (At left, courtesy John D. Brown; below author's collection.)

Penguins Arrive. The owner of the MV *Victoria*, Capt. Matt Monise Sr., took very good care of these penguins from the Galapagos Islands and delivered them to the new San Diego Zoo complete with names, Betsy and Bell. Portuguese captains and crews had a respect for the zoo's ideology and made significant contributions to the animal collections. (Courtesy of Phyllis Rose.)

Southern Pacific Seaplane, 1957. The *Southern Pacific* became the first American tuna clipper conversion and had the addition of a seaplane. This 123-foot wooden tuna clipper was built by J. M. Martinac shipbuilding in Tacoma, Washington, for owner and captain Lou Brito. The conversion from a tuna clipper to a purse seiner changed fishing technology from pole fishing to nylon nets with power blocks. A total of 75 boats made the conversions to seiners.

THE BROTHERHOOD OF THE MERMAID. Crew members who remain out to sea for considerable weeks at a time depend on the allegiances made during the fishing process. As men work closely together to perform daily hazardous duties, all facets of their lives become intertwined. A crew consists of a captain, navigator, chief engineer, deck boss, cook, and crew members. Several of the crew members in this photograph remained lifelong friends. Pictured from left to right are (first row) Leo Correia, Johnny "Sugar" Correia, and Wendell Neves; (second row) unidentified, Joe Caboz, John Neves, Gilbert "Gibby" Frank, and Manuel "Maxi" Lira. (Courtesy of Gayle Frank.)

COLLECTING BAIT. Clipper boats depended on bait to draw the tuna near the vessel. As the crew throws bait into the water, the men on the poles pull the tuna in. The bait net is a miniature round net that can be drawn up into a purse and brought alongside the boat to the fishing grounds. This wonderful image shows the coordinated effort it takes to harvest the bait out of the net.

THE BIG CATCH. This alleyway filled with tuna is a fisherman's dream. Many tuna clippers were manned by crews of fathers, sons, brothers, relatives, and friends. A catch like this meant a prosperous year for everyone. This large catch is ready to be loaded in the hold and followed by a great night's sleep for the crew.

FILLING THE HOLDS. After the handling of the bait, the holds were cleaned out and prepared for the tuna. Filling the holds with seawater and additional salt brought down the temperature to freezing. When the tuna finally froze, the saltwater was pumped out and dry frozen tuna was left in the hold. This made the boat lighter and stabilized the vessel. Wells, or holds, had different capacities depending on the vessel and had to be packed tight with ice to protect the fish and yield a good market.

LAUNCHING OF THE *SOUTH SEAS*, 1958. The launching of a fishing vessel is a sight to behold. Built for Vincent Gann, the *South Seas* hits the water with a velocity that is clearly illustrated in the images on these two pages. Notice the angle at which the boat breaks the surface of the water.

A Launch and a View from Above. As the *South Seas* hits the water, it creates enormous waves. This vessel made many trips to Magdalena Bay, fishing for bait in Baja California and the eastern tropical Pacific waters. At right, Capt. Lionel Vargas is seen up in the crow's nest scouting for fish. (At right, courtesy of Lionel Vargas.)

FISHING HARDWARE. Many types of fishing hardware are needed to protect and assist the crew for a safe and prosperous trip. In the early days, boats had no weather systems and relied only on the decisions of the captain and interpretations of the weather. The image at left shows a very dependable tool—the large binoculars required to locate large schools of tuna. Below, the diving helmet was also an important piece of equipment that allowed crew members to submerge under water with only a rubber hose connected to the helmet. A hand pump on deck supplied air while the divers worked the net around the bait and brought it to the surface. (At left, courtesy of Gayle Frank; below, Virginia Correia.)

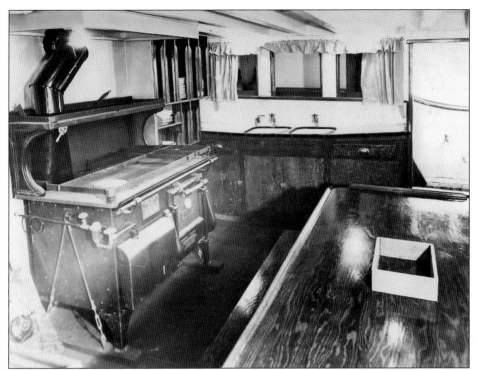

THE GALLEY. The above 1930s image is of a typical galley on a tuna clipper. These vessels had small areas to prepare and eat meals or to congregate after a hard day's work. The cast iron stove seen here was state of the art in its day. On occasion, boats were out during the holidays and not able to make it home to port. The crew below has gathered on Christmas day to make a toast to good fortune and ask God's blessing for their families who await their return from the sea. (Both courtesy of Virginia Correia.)

BLESSING OF THE BOAT. Portuguese fishermen, being very religious, always had blessings before a launching. Bishop Buddy is depicted blessing this tuna clipper while family and friends are gathered. It was also customary to have an altar inside the boat to provide the men a reserved place to pray. (Courtesy of Virginia Correia.)

TUNA BOAT ASSOCIATION, 1950S. This organization was developed by the tuna vessel owners to protect the American tuna fishermen's rights by offering an opportunity for negotiations with Latin American nations. Seen here are the charter members at their Christmas party. Pictured, in no certain order, are Pete Zalinski, Frank Gonsalves, Matt Monise, John Cardosa, Manuel Frietas, Harold "Pop" Morgan, Harold Cary, Manuel Rosa, Guy Silva, Bill Hoss, M. O. Medina, Joe Rodgers, Louis Defalco, Anthony "Hank" Madruga, Louis Castagnola, Frank Perry, George Campbell, Ed Madruga, Vernon Brown, and Frank Gonsalves.

THE FLEET IS IN FOR CHRISTMAS, 1947. The fleet is in for Christmas at San Diego Marine Construction. The two vessels on the right have been returned to their owners after being requisitioned in World War II as YP vessels. They are being torn up and reconditioned for tuna fishing. This commanding and unusual photograph shows the fleet in its grandeur.

TEAMWORK. Joe "Zamato" Luis (left) and Manuel "Vasco" Caboz (right) are working hard to pull in the net together with great teamwork. It was not uncommon to travel as far as Africa, Panama, Puerto Rico, Ecuador, and the eastern or western Pacific in pursuit of tuna. These men both went on to become successful captains and boat owners.

93

HIGH SEAS CANNERY. In the early 1900s, San Diego tuna vessels had no refrigeration to keep the fish fresh, so canneries set up canner stations along the Baja coast. Boats were now able to drop

THE FRENCH SARDINE COMPANY, 1900s. The first cannery in Point Loma specializing in fancy French-style sardines, the French Sardine Company, was built by Alexander Steele and Edward Hume. Sardines quickly became obsolete as Americans began to buy tuna as a cheap staple. The sign on the right reminds one of the once-plentiful bounty San Diego Bay held. (Courtesy of Virginia Correia.)

off a day's catch and continue fishing. The capability to freeze fish and ship them in containers to San Diego allowed boats to stay in the fishing grounds. (Courtesy of Delores Madruga.)

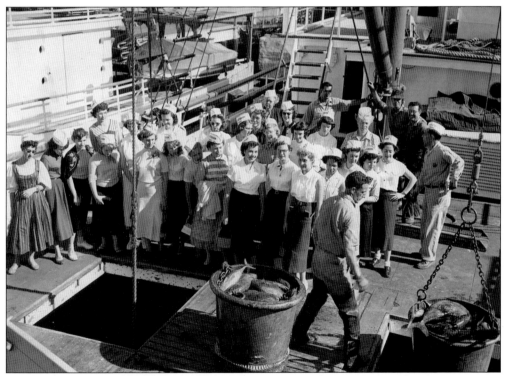

SUN HARBOR CANNERY. Women working in the cannery are seen here wearing their Breast of Chicken cannery hats. Large containers are being hoisted up from the well to retrieve the tuna. Often these ladies were invited to lunch after inspecting the fresh catch of the day. (Courtesy of Virginia Correia.)

MV HORNET. This boat was built in Washington state by the Tacoma Shipbuilders Company for Capt. A. Roland Virissimo, Manuel Falante, and Del Monte. This vessel was the first San Diego tuna seiner to be built from the keel up. The *Hornet* is shown in Puget Sound on its maiden voyage. (Courtesy of Louise Virissimo.)

MV SEA QUEST, 1970. Built for owner Manuel Silva by San Diego Marine, the *Sea Quest* was the third 750-ton vessel to be constructed at that time. The *Sea Quest* is pictured here on the San Diego Bay, where many mothers, wives, and daughters have fond memories of greeting their loved ones returning from the sea. (Courtesy of Capt. Rick Virissimo.)

KING OSCAR. Built by the Campbell Shipyard, this boat had a 1,200-ton capacity. Capt. Johnny Gois is one of the men who owned and ran this boat, but often a tuna seiner had many different captains over the course of its existence. The angle of this shot is rare and shows the net being pulled up by the wench. (Courtesy of Jimmy Lira Jr.)

MEDINA PANEL. Tuna fishing is associated with the porpoise in the eastern tropical Pacific Ocean, where the mammals and tuna migrate together. In order to harvest tuna without harming porpoises, a new technology called the Medina Panel was created by Capt. Harold Medina. A superior nylon net made with a smaller mesh panel allowed porpoises to be released during the new back-down method. (Courtesy of Jimmy Lira Jr.)

A FISHERMAN AND HIS NET, C. 1960. Manuel G. Balelo is pictured on the San Diego's Embarcadero while he is methodically sewing a fishing net. Born on Christmas Eve, 1900, he emigrated from Paul do Mar, Madeira, to the United States in his early teens. After working the railroads in Lowell, Massachusetts, Manuel came to San Diego to fish for tuna. This outstanding image represents the heart and soul of a tuna fisherman whose life belonged to the sea. (Courtesy of Louise Virissimo.)

TUNAMAN'S MEMORIAL, 1986. The *Tunaman's Memorial* statue was created by sculptor Franco Vianella and established by Anthony and John Mascarenhas and John Rebelo. The concept for the statue arose from the idea that the San Diego fishermen should be recognized for their contributions and enrichments to the tuna industry. Citizens in the community also donated money to help fund the memorial on Shelter Island Drive in Point Loma. The memorial is dedicated to "honoring those who built an industry and remembering those who left this harbor in the sun never to return."

Five

THE PORTUGUESE
PROUDLY SERVE

CHRISTENING OF *SERVICE*, C.
1940. In 1941, commercial
fishermen were requested
to assist in the fight for
freedom with the U.S.
Navy in World War II. Six
hundred men volunteered
and received warrant
ratings to serve as part of
crews on the powerful YP
boats converted from tuna
clippers. Portuguese men
also proudly served their
country for generations
in many branches of the
military. During World
War I, World War II, the
Korean War, and Vietnam,
they were seen in their
uniforms fighting for
liberty. Many lost their
lives, and some will never
forget the cost of freedom.

SGT. ANTONE ROSE, 1943. Serving in the U.S. Army, Antone Rose (left) became a part of the Rainbow Infantry tank destroyer unit. In 1944, he went missing in action and became a prisoner of war in Germany. After his return to his unit, Antone received several medals, two of which were the Purple Heart and Bronze Star. Shown below are the German prisoner-of-war papers confiscated by the Americans when the camp was liberated. Notice "RC" for Roman Catholic and "Fisherman" as his occupation. (Both courtesy of Phyllis Rose.)

THE COMPANY WILL APPRECIATE SUGGESTIONS FROM ITS PATRONS CONCERNING ITS SERVICE

1	2	3	4	5	6	7	8	9	10	11	12	13	14	15	16	17	18	19	20	21	22	23	24	25

Perſonalkarte I: perſonelle Angaben

Beſchriftung der Erkennungsmarke:
Nr. *078212*

Kriegsgefangenen-Stammlager: *XIIA*

Lager: *XIIA*

Name: *ROSE*

Staatsangehörigkeit: *USA*   O

Vorname: *ANTONE*

Dienſtgrad: *SGT*

Geburtstag und -ort: *12-10-22 – CALIF*

Truppenteil: *ARMY*   Komp. uſw.:

Religion: *R·C*

Zivilberuf: *FISHERMAN*   Berufs-Gr.:

Matrikel Nr. (Stammrolle des Heimatstaates): *3827774*

Vorname des Vaters: *JOE*

Gefangennahme (Ort und Datum): *GERMANY 7*

Familienname der Mutter:

Ob gesund, krank, verwundet eingeliefert: *FIT*

Lichtbild | Nähere Perſonalbeſchreibung:

Größe | Haarfarbe | Beſondere Kennzeichen:
5-0 | *BLACK* |

Fingerabdruck des rechten Zeigefingers | Name und Anſchrift der zu benachrichtigenden Perſon in der Heimat des Kriegsgefangenen

MRS· D· SILVEYRA
3226 FENELON
SAN·DIEGO – CALIF

078212 XIIA

100

A FAMILY SERVES, C. 1940.
Mr. and Mrs. Lira had five sons, four of whom served in the U.S. military. In the image at right, two sons are home on leave visiting their parents. Pictured from left to right are (sitting) Manuel and Louisa Lira; (standing) Pvt. Raul Lira and Seaman Jimmy Lira, U.S. Coast Guard. It is easy to see the patriotism Portuguese Americans have and the pride parents had for their sons. Note Mrs. Lira's smile as she wears her son's Dixie cup hat and Mr. Lira's pride as he dons his son's garrison cap. Below, Seaman John Lira (left) and Pvt. Tony Lira (right), who served in the Korean War, pose for military portraits. (Both courtesy of Mary Pereira.)

BOILERMAN'S MATE 2ND CLASS MATTEO BALLATORE, U.S. NAVY RESERVE, C. 1945. "Gilmore," as his friends called him, was attached to the APA-198 transport ship division. While serving during the Okinawa invasion, Gilmore drove amphibious boats with troops up onto the beach. After arriving home, Gilmore met his daughter Barbara for the first time. Five days later, he met with tragedy and suddenly died from complications while serving in the war at Oakland Naval Hospital. Gilmore was loved by all who knew him. (Courtesy of Rita Ballatore.)

SEAMEN JOHN BROWN AND WENDALL NEVES, 1952. In the U.S. Navy, John served in the Korean War on the renowned battleship USS *Iowa*. On a port stop in Yokosuka, Japan, John (left) and best buddy Wendell Neves, who was serving in the U.S. Coast Guard, are seen posing for a leave photograph. Both became active members of the Portuguese community. They are 1948 graduates of Point Loma High School and remain friends today. (Courtesy of John D. Brown.)

PVT. EDUENNO ALVES, C. 1940. Enlisting in the U.S. military at the age of 16, Eddie (left) is seen with an army buddy while relaxing on leave at the barracks at Fort Bragg, North Carolina. He served as a paratrooper in the renowned 82nd Airborne infantry division during World War II and was a merchant marine stationed in Pearl Harbor as well. He then became an accomplished chief engineer for the American tuna industry. (Courtesy of Aldina Alves.)

SGT. MANUEL BALELO, 1952. The son of Adam and Mary Francisco Balelo, Manuel served in the U.S. Air Force and was attached to the 308th Squadron. After serving his country, he became a commercial tuna fisherman from 1956 until he retired in 1988. Currently he resides with his wife, Pulqueria, in San Diego. (Courtesy of Delores Madruga.)

DAVID GONSALVES, C. 1960. During the Vietnam War, David boldly served his unit in the U.S. Army and obtained a serious injury from a land mine risking his life to save others. Returning home a decorated hero, he received the Purple Heart and Bronze Star. David remains humble about his service to his country. (Courtesy of Belmira Gonsalves.)

CREW OF THE USS CHAMBERLIN, 1942. The U.S. Navy realized the significant importance of the tuna clippers' ability to maneuver in shallow or dangerous areas and deliver perishables, transport troops, and pull fallen pilots from the sea. This crew poses on the *Chamberlin* before its christening.

TUNA CLIPPERS SERVE, 1943. Pictured above with the 11th Naval District port director's office are tuna skippers and officers, from left to right, (first row) Machinist John Turner, Boatswain Edward Madruga, U.S. Navy Reserve Machinist Manuel Enrique, retired U.S. Navy Comdr. W. J. Morcott, retired U.S. Navy Lt. J. F. Piotrowski, retired U.S. Navy Lt. Comdr. J. E. Kemmer, and U.S. Navy Reserve Boatswains E. Varley and E. Qualin; (second row) Boatswains Victor Rosa and Frank Gonsalves; Ens. Antiono Mascarenhas, Boatswain John Tosso; Machinists Robert Hargreaves, James Burk, Mike Ascuitto, V. I. Simian, W. A. Robbins, and L. E. Wiley. All of the sailors in the second row were naval reservists. Below, a full YP crew poses on the ship's deck.

MV MARINER. The *Mariner* was built in 1928 and later became known as the *Patria*. On December 9, 1941, it was acquired by the U.S. Navy as YP-234. This is one of the oldest-recorded tuna vessels used for YP service that also returned to the fleet after the war. (Courtesy of Lionel Vargas.)

YMS-475, 1944. This launching photograph was taken of a navy vessel on June 5 by San Diego Marine Construction Company, one of the oldest marine facilities in San Diego that is still in existence today. Tuna fisherman depended on facilities like this to keep up their tuna clippers and supply various needs. YP boats and naval vessels were painted gunmetal grey, and guns were added as a new shield of protection. Cannons and machine guns were also added, and a naval gunner's mate was assigned to the boat to educate the crew and watch the armor.

THE NORMANDIE SERVES, 1942. The tuna clipper *Normandie* is shown here converted to YP-291, with her stacks revealing eight red chevrons for wartime service. Tony Mascarenhas was given orders to serve on this vessel as an officer. Out of 33 tuna clippers acquired for YP service, 2 were not sold back to their former owners.

CONTE GRAND, YP-520. Three YP vessels were lost following a typhoon in Okinawa, Japan, in October 1945. On October 7, the *Paramount* (YP-289) and the *Conte Grand* (YP-520), pictured here, were beached on a sandbar. On October 9, the *Challenger* (YP-239) was lost due to a tropical storm.

WE'RE IN THE NAVY NOW. These three YP servicemen are pictured having a ball in a local watering hole. From left to right are Joaquin Quallin, Johnny Luz, and Joe Madruga. Joe was credited as the youngest chief warrant officer in the navy. In 1940, Eddie Madruga became master of the *Paramount*, and he took the boat into World War II as an YP vessel with his brother Joe. The *Paramount* unfortunately sank in a typhoon off Okinawa in 1945. During the course of their service, these "yippies" faced adversity and gained the respect of the U.S. Navy. (Courtesy of João's Tin Fish—Mike Alves.)

PORTUGUESE PATRIOTISM. Uncle Sam and Lady Liberty head up this group of young boys carrying a grand American flag during the Portuguese parade.

THE YP MONUMENT DEDICATION, 2008. It took years of hard work for the YP Monument to become a reality. With the generous and relentless help of August Felando, Kenny Alameda, Julius Zolezzi, John Rebelo, and the Port of San Diego, the YP tuna fleet has finally been honored and recognized. On June 28, a dedication authenticated the memorial (below), and it was finally unveiled with a beautiful ceremony from the port district. Three friends from their YP days were reunited after 60 years at the ceremony and posed for a photograph (right). From left to right, Joe Madruga, Vito Sardo, and Pete Bosnich take a moment to reminisce over old times.

"V" Is for Victory, 1945. Phyllis Monise Rose was given the honor of portraying Miss Victory during the 1945 festa. This was the last festa she participated in, as she was 17, the typical end of festa participation for most youths. She is shown in a white dress holding her victory letter with great pride. Her future husband, Antone Rose, received the Purple Heart and Bronze Star for his service in World War II. (Courtesy of Phyllis Rose.)

Six

A Spirit
of Community

THE KELLOGG'S GANG, C. 1930. Beaches have been a source of enjoyment for Point Loma residents for many years. Kellogg's Beach is located in the La Playa area and still remains a favorite spot to relax. These Portuguese children are enjoying the quiet shore and calm waters in the bay while posing for a photograph in front of the Peckham Pier. From left to right are Arnold Monise, Edmund Freitas, Manuel Freitas Jr., Wendall Fernandes, two Stanton girls, Matilda Tavares, and Armand Tavares.

CABRILHO'S FIRST LANDING, 1892. Manuel Cabral, a prominent citizen and fisherman in the Roseville area, was the first to portray Cabrilho in a reenactment of his historical landing in 1542. This 350th anniversary celebration took place at Broadway Pier and was complete with marching bands parading up Broadway Street to Horton Plaza. Cabral's costume, reminiscent of the 16th century, was comprised of velvet knickers and an ostrich feather hat. Cabral became a specimen collector for what would become the Scripps-Birch Aquarium and continued as an oceanic collector for many years. A plaque on display at the aquarium honors his contributions.

THE CORONADO FERRY, 1915. The Star Line Crescent Ferry was established for citizens to travel between Coronado Island and La Playa. Portuguese families enjoyed the relaxing ferry ride to Coronado along with the electric streetcar, which transported them to Tent City for a day of leisure. Notice the all the derbies and the fancy hats women would adorn for a day's outing.

THE GIRLS' DAY AT THE BEACH, C. 1930. La Jolla Beach was a favorite place for these ladies to go for a day of fun and relaxation. The Portuguese communities had groups of very close neighbors and relatives. Enjoying this beautiful summer day from left to right are Hazel Vargus, May Mitchell, Mary E. Brown, Alja Silva, Mrs. Silva, Aldina Brown (little girl in front), Mrs. Adelitha Valin, and Mrs. Nunes. (Courtesy of Aldina Alves.)

CATCH OF THE DAY, 1936. Ed Boilard, a local photographer, took this picture of young boys at a cannery in Point Loma. These kids all learned the trade of fishing by helping their fathers, grandfathers, and uncles as they came of age. Here the boys proudly display the catch of the day. Pictured in no particular order are Frankie Correia, Arnold Cardoza, John Cardoza, Eddie Correia, Manuel Ferreira, Albert Correia, Edmond Cardoza, Albert Ferreira, Manuel Pestana, and Johnny Correia. (Courtesy of Virginia Correia.)

THE CALIFORNIA PACIFIC INTERNATIONAL EXPOSITION, 1935–1936. During the Depression, the expo was held to boost the local economy. Inspired by the new idea, the Portuguese came out to see all that Balboa Park had to offer. On September 29, a Portuguese day at the exhibition was sponsored by the Portuguese American League. The consul from Washington, D.C., was the guest of the House of Portugal. Dancers dressed up to support the Portuguese exhibit. Here the Brown (De Brum) family poses in front of the historic botanical gardens, one of the largest lath structures in the world, which dates back to 1915. (Courtesy of John D. Brown.)

THE FIRST PORTUGUESE AMERICAN DANCERS, 1954. To preserve Portuguese heritage and traditions and bring unity, the dancers became a performing group for festas and religious and cultural events. Started by Mary Monise, the dancers are still performing today, with the addition of a junior group as well. They are seen here at a performance at Balboa Park. From left to right are (first row) Edna and Tony Madruga, Deutilde Varley, and João Simas; (second row) Mr. and Mrs. Dennis Oliver, Aurora Gamma, Machado Medina, Mr. and Mrs. Jack Theodore, Mary and Tony Monise, Doris Oliver-Porto, Lawrence Oliver, Maria Rita Rosa, and Antonio Rosa.

THE POINT LOMA STRINGS. This group of Portuguese men was formed to entertain and preserve traditional Portuguese music and folklore. Entertaining at festas, hall events, and cultural fairs, the strings have also played for the Smithsonian Institution's bicentennial celebration in Washington, D.C. Pictured here from left to right are Manuel Frizado Silva, Leonel Garcia da Rosa, Antonio Garces da Rosa, and Manuel Labrincha performing in front of San Diego's county administration building.

AMALIA RODRIGUES, C. 1940. Performing at the U.P.S.E.S. Hall, Amalia came to delight the audience with her *fado* (Portuguese ballad) style of music. She acquired a worldwide audience, and it was an honor to watch her perform before Point Lomas Portuguese fans. Delores Balelo Madruga came to enjoy the concert and caught this quick photograph of her favorite star. (Courtesy of Delores Madruga.)

DANA JUNIOR HIGH SCHOOL, APRIL 2, 1946. Richard Henry Dana Jr. High was named after the author who wrote *Two Years before the Mast* and was designed to double as a cold war bomb shelter. Dana's doors originally opened in 1928 and became the junior high school, serving grades

CABRILLO SCHOOL, 1939. Cabrillo Elementary School is located at 3120 Talbot Street and has been serving the Portuguese community for 103 years. The school was originally named Roseville School and was changed to Point Loma Elementary in 1921. To avoid confusion when Point Loma High School was built in 1925, it was renamed after the Portuguese explorer João Rodrigues Cabrilho. Members of the graduating class of 1939 take a moment to pose for this picture. (Courtesy of Marge Medina Amptman.)

116

seven through nine for the Portuguese families in the area. This impressive panorama illustrates the vast number of neighborhood children at that time. Seen here is the ninth-grade graduating class of 1946. (Courtesy of John D. Brown.)

THE POINTERS, C. 1940. Point Loma High School was dedicated in 1925, and the first graduating class consisted of seven students who celebrated their commencement at Balboa Park. Point Loma High is now the third-largest high school in the San Diego Unified School District. Don Larson became the school's claim to fame when he pitched a no-hitter in the 1947 World Series. Seen here from left to right are song leaders Joyce Simms, Jeanne Lee Miller, and Thelma Fintzelberg providing lots of school spirit for the football game. (Courtesy of Shirley Virissimo.)

BEACH PYRAMIDS, C. 1940. It was common to see local kids having fun at La Jolla Shores Beach and forming three-tier pyramids. The boys always provided the foundation, and the girls loved it. These neighborhood friends gathered on weekends, and their friendships have endured to this day. (Courtesy of Frank family.)

THE BEACH BOYS, C. 1940. This beachfront scene captures, from left to right, Manuel Coito, Jack Dutra, Eddie Correia, Tony Rodrigues, and Anibal Freitas horsing around at Mission Beach. This was a great place for the high school kids to socialize. Eddie went on to become part owner of the *Helen S.* tuna boat with family members. (Courtesy of Virginia Correia.)

BATHING BEAUTIES.
This 1950s
Oldsmobile proudly
shows off two young
girls who became
sisters-in-law and
best friends. Aldina
Brown (left) and
Jeanne Lee Miller
both married tuna
fishermen and
raised sons who
followed in the
fishing industry,
which was a typical
lifestyle in their era.
(Courtesy of Donna
Alves-Calhoun and
Shirley Virissimo.)

THE GIRLS AT MISSION BEACH, 1948. Old Mission Beach became a spot where high school kids met on the weekends. Three Portuguese girls, (from left to right) Eileen Vargas, Vera Fernandes, and Lucille Cardozo, show off their flamingo bathing suits while relaxing at the beach and enjoying a picnic outing. Lucille married fisherman and accomplished mandolin player Sal Freitas. (Courtesy of Sal and Lucille Freitas.)

BOYS' NIGHT OUT, c. 1940. Ollie Virissimo, Johnny Correia, Frank Correia Sr., and Johnny Carvalho are having fun at a nightclub and are ready for a night on the town. All of these men followed the tradition of fishing, which was very prevalent in their day. (Courtesy of Virginia Correia.)

THE PORTUGUESE "GUNGA," 1949. These young men are ready for the festa and obviously having a great time posing in front of a 1949 Pontiac convertible. Most of these men grew up together and attended the same schools and community events. Shown here from left to right are (first row, kneeling) Arnold Freitas; (second row) Ralph Rosa, "Little Zip" Dores, Johnny Carvalho, Sal Freitas, Eddie Alves, Art Silva, John "Brut" Brum, and Arnold Mitchell; (third row) Harry Carvalho and Ed Brown. (Courtesy of Sal and Lucille Freitas.)

ROSE'S VARIETY STORE, C. 1940. A popular hangout for young adults after Sunday mass, Rose's had all the household necessities. Georgie's Fountain Lunch Counter was the café to dine in and show off fancy hats and dresses. Frank Rose, owner of Merit Variety Store, was originally from Hanford, California, and of Portuguese descent. Virginia Brown Correia was hired as his first counter girl. Striking a pose are, from left to right, Lucy Brenha, Mary Brito, Hazel Virissimo, and Mary Brenha. (Courtesy of Virginia Correia.)

SCHOOL BOYS, C. 1940. Morris Souza, Anthony Silva, Al Holbrook, and unidentified are waiting for the girls after Sunday mass. Zell's Grocery and Point Loma Café were located on Rosecrans Street facing north. Notice the old post office, which is now located around the corner on Cannon Street. (Courtesy of Virginia Correia.)

THE ROSE PARADE, 2008. The Rose Parade got a taste of Portugal, and it was a wonderful sight to see. The Portuguese American community was invited to participate for the first time in the 119th Pasadena Tournament of Roses Parade. Emeril Lagasse is also a proud Portuguese American and was chosen to be master of ceremonies for the parade as well. San Diego's Donald Valadao was chosen to depict the Portuguese navigator João Rodrigues Cabrilho.

ROMARIAS. The Romaria originated in the Madeira Islands and is celebrated on Christmas Eve in church. A procession of singing angels leads Portuguese singing groups to the altar. A replica fishing boat, or *barca*, is promised in memory of a loved one and wheeled up to the altar with gifts. Mass is celebrated following the singing. The celebration continues the day after Christmas, when gifts are auctioned off and the proceeds are given to the church. Pictured among the group, from left to right are (far left) Veronica Falante and Maria (Faneca) Rodrigues; (far right) Malecas Rodrigues, Belmira Gonsalves, and Joe Pequeno; (in front) Mary Jo and Sweety Gonsalves.

BING CROSBY. San Diego's tuna clipper *Golden Gate* got a taste of Hollywood when Bing Crosby and Andy Divine chartered the boat for a day of sportfishing. Capt. Frank Perry took the famous cargo out on August 18, 1938, and as one can see in this great photograph, it was a good day.

SAN DIEGO TUNA CLIPPER
GOLDEN GATE
CAPTAIN FRANK PERRY

ANDY DIVINE & BING CROSBY
AUGUST 18TH 1938

Chubasco
High adventure on the high seas
with the great tuna fleet—
and the boy who
had a chip on both shoulders
and dared the world to knock it off.

RICHARD CHRISTOPHER   SUSAN   ANN
EGAN · JONES · STRASBERG · SOTHERN OAKLAND · TOTTER · FOSTER · WHITNEY
WILLIAM CONRAD ALLEN H. MINER TECHNICOLOR® PANAVISION® FROM WARNER BROS.-SEVEN ARTS

CHUBASCO, 1968. This movie captured San Diego's Portuguese tuna fishing community. It was filmed in Point Loma and the downtown areas using local boats such as the *Bernadette*. In this film, a troubled young man is ordered to serve time on a tuna clipper instead of going to jail. *Tuna Clipper* (1949), starring Roddy McDowell, was another tuna fishing movie shot in San Diego.

FIRST CABRILLO QUEEN, 1964. Nancy Hollerbach, a native of San Diego, was chosen as the first Miss Cabrillo sponsored by the United Portuguese Americans. A celebration at the U. S. Grant Hotel was held with a dinner dance. Nancy then went on to place third in a statewide competition on September 12 at the California State Fair in Sacramento.

FILARMONICA UNIÃO PORTUGUESA DE SAN DIEGO, C. 1970. More commonly known as a marching band, this musical tradition has been brought from the Azores Islands. These bands date back over 100 years and are a treasure to the community for their active participation. Traditionally they were predominantly male musicians, but currently women are allowed to perform. Pictured here are the San Diego band and its board, from left to right in the first row, Fatima Estrela, Carlos Silva, Evelina DaRosa, Christian Da Rosa, Gilberto Rosa, Carlos Pereira, Theresa Medina Carillo, and Joe Silva. (Courtesy of Carlos Pereira.)

ALLIANCA AZOREANA. This alliance was founded to represent the interest of the Azorean emigrants with the Portuguese government in Portugal. After the government stabilized itself, the club then became a social alliance that welcomes Azoreans as well as anyone interested in being a member. Pictured are the charter members along with the executive board, including president Paulo R. Goulart (second from right), vice president Jose Mauricio Lomelino Alves (far right), and secretary Olina Bertao Dias Arnold (center, in the skirt). (Courtesy of Elsa Machado.)

PORTUGUESE AMERICAN DANCERS, 2007. This dance group was formed by Mary Monise and has continued for over 50 years. These authentic handmade costumes are purchased in Portugal and passed down to future dancers. The Portuguese American Dance group participates in many community events and competes in annual folkloric competitions. The youth today are encouraged to receive a college education with diverse community involvement. (Courtesy of Portuguese American Dancers.)

THE FIRST LADY OF THE HALL. Mary Alice Gonsalves became director and the first woman elected president, in 1985, to the U.P.S.E.S. organization, which is over 100 years old. Pictured here, Mary Alice is recognized by the Portuguese American Leadership Council of the United States (PALCUS) for businesswoman of the year in 2009 and became festa president with her husband, Avelino, in 1988. In 2009, the Portuguese Historical Center honored Mary Alice for businesswoman of the year as well.

THE FRATERNALS. These organizations were started to offer life insurance policies to help Portuguese American families and give assistance to the less fortunate during the Depression. A fun social setting was also incorporated to boost the spirits of the members. Some of the fraternal organizations are Divine Holy Spirit (D.E.S.), Brotherhood of the Divine Holy Spirit (I.D.E.S.), S.P.R.S.I., and U.P.P.E.C. The U.P.S.E.S. float is seen here at the festa with Mrs. Medina, wife of the first supreme president, and friends. (Courtesy of Barbara Hosaka.)

PORTUGUESE HISTORICAL CENTER (PHC), 2009. Founded in 1977 by Basilio Freitas along with other community citizens, the PHC became one of the first organizations of its kind in the United States. It exists to archive history and to provide a record for posterity. Its purpose is to educate others about the role the Portuguese have played in San Diego and around the world. The 2009 PHC Board of Directors poses here. Pictured from left to right are (first row) vice president Rosemarie Silva and president Therese Garces; (second row) Barbara Moffat, Aldina Alves, Shirley Virissimo, treasurer Daniel Silva, secretary Diana Balelo, Caprice Ribeiro, Donna Alves-Calhoun, and Jordan Laubach; (not pictured) president emeritus Mary Giglitto, parliamentarian Virginia Correia, and Andrea Da Luz.

WHAT A GREAT RIDE. The Portuguese American community of San Diego has come a long way, from the simple La Playa community to the powerful days of the tuna industry. Today its heritage is protected and cherished. Manuel Soares is seen riding in his touring car in 1915. Bom viagem!

ACROSS AMERICA, PEOPLE ARE DISCOVERING SOMETHING WONDERFUL. *THEIR HERITAGE.*

Arcadia Publishing is the leading local history publisher in the United States. With more than 5,000 titles in print and hundreds of new titles released every year, Arcadia has extensive specialized experience chronicling the history of communities and celebrating America's hidden stories, bringing to life the people, places, and events from the past. To discover the history of other communities across the nation, please visit:

www.arcadiapublishing.com

Customized search tools allow you to find regional history books about the town where you grew up, the cities where your friends and family live, the town where your parents met, or even that retirement spot you've been dreaming about.